PRACTICAL DATABASE PROGRAMMING WITH SQL AND PL/SQL

SIVAKUMAR, R.D.

ISBN: 978-93-340-5243-5

CONTENTS
SQL

PL/SQL

SQL

Create a Table

```
CREATE TABLE employees (
   employee_id NUMBER PRIMARY KEY,
   first_name VARCHAR2(50),
   last_name VARCHAR2(50),
   email VARCHAR2(100),
   department_id NUMBER,
   salary NUMBER
);
```

Insert Data into a Table

```
INSERT INTO employees (employee_id, first_name, last_name, email,
department_id, salary)
VALUES (101, 'John', 'Doe', 'jdoe@example.com', 10, 50000);
```

Select Data from a Table

Update Data in a Table

```
UPDATE employees SET department_id = 20 WHERE employee_id = 101;
```

Delete Data from a Table

```
DELETE FROM employees WHERE employee_id = 101;
```

Use WHERE Clause for Filtering

```
SELECT * FROM employees WHERE department_id = 10;
```

Use ORDER BY Clause for Sorting

```
SELECT * FROM employees ORDER BY last_name ASC;
```

Use GROUP BY Clause for Aggregation

```
SELECT department_id, COUNT(*) as employee_count
FROM employees
GROUP BY department_id;
```

Use JOIN to Combine Tables

```
SELECT e.first_name, e.last_name, d.department_name
FROM employees e
INNER JOIN departments d ON e.department_id = d.department_id;
```

Use Subqueries

```
SELECT * FROM employees WHERE department_id IN (SELECT
department_id FROM departments WHERE location_id = 1700);
```

Create Views

```
CREATE VIEW department_10_employees AS
SELECT * FROM employees WHERE department_id = 10;
```

Create Indexes

```
CREATE INDEX idx_lastname ON employees(last_name);
```

Create Sequences

```
CREATE SEQUENCE emp_id_seq START WITH 1001 INCREMENT BY 1;
```

Use Constraints (NOT NULL, UNIQUE, PRIMARY KEY, FOREIGN KEY)

```
ALTER TABLE employees ADD CONSTRAINT pk_employee_id PRIMARY
KEY (employee_id);
ALTER TABLE employees ADD CONSTRAINT fk_department_id FOREIGN
KEY (department_id) REFERENCES departments(department_id);
```

Use ALTER TABLE to Add a Column

```
ALTER TABLE employees ADD (birthdate DATE);
```

Use ALTER TABLE to Modify a Column

```
ALTER TABLE employees MODIFY (salary NUMBER(10,2));
```

Use ALTER TABLE to Drop a Column

```
ALTER TABLE employees DROP COLUMN email;
```

Use COMMIT to Save Transactions

```
COMMIT;
```

Use ROLLBACK to Undo Transactions

```
ROLLBACK;
```

Use Savepoints

```
SAVEPOINT sp1;
```

Use TRUNCATE to Empty a Table

```
TRUNCATE TABLE employees;
```

Use DROP TABLE to Remove a Table

```
DROP TABLE employees;
```

Use TRUNCATE vs. DELETE

```
TRUNCATE TABLE employees; – Removes all rows and resets storage
DELETE FROM employees; -- Removes all rows but doesn't reset storage
```

Use COUNT() Function

```
SELECT COUNT(*) FROM employees;
```

Use SUM() Function

```
SELECT SUM(salary) FROM employees;
```

Use AVG() Function

Use MAX() and MIN() Functions

Use HAVING Clause with Aggregate Function

```
SELECT department_id, AVG(salary) AS avg_salary FROM employees
```

```
GROUP BY department_id
HAVING AVG(salary) > 50000;
```

Use IN Operator

```
SELECT *
FROM employees
WHERE department_id IN (10, 20);
```

Use BETWEEN Operator

```
SELECT *
FROM employees
WHERE hire_date BETWEEN TO_DATE('2022-01-01', 'YYYY-MM-DD') AND
TO_DATE('2022-12-31', 'YYYY-MM-DD');
```

Use LIKE Operator

```
SELECT *
FROM employees
WHERE last_name LIKE 'S%';
```

Use DISTINCT Keyword

```
SELECT DISTINCT job_id
FROM employees;
```

Use UNION Operator

```
SELECT employee_id, first_name
FROM employees
WHERE department_id = 10
UNION
SELECT employee_id, first_name
FROM employees
WHERE department_id = 20;
```

Use INTERSECT Operator

```
SELECT employee_id, first_name
FROM employees
WHERE department_id = 10
INTERSECT
SELECT employee_id, first_name
FROM employees
WHERE job_id = 'MANAGER';
```

Use MINUS Operator

```
SELECT employee_id, first_name
FROM employees
WHERE department_id = 10
MINUS
SELECT employee_id, first_name
FROM employees
WHERE job_id = 'CLERK';
```

Use Substitution Variables (&)

```
ACCEPT department_id NUMBER PROMPT 'Enter Department ID: '
SELECT *
FROM employees
WHERE department_id = &department_id;
```

Use Analytic Functions (ROW_NUMBER, RANK, DENSE_RANK)

```
SELECT employee_id, first_name, salary,
    ROW_NUMBER() OVER (PARTITION BY department_id ORDER BY
salary DESC) AS emp_rank
FROM employees;
```

Use NVL() Function

```
SELECT first_name, NVL(commission_pct, 0) AS commission_pct FROM
```

```
employees;
```

Use CASE Statement

```
SELECT employee_id, first_name,
     CASE
        WHEN salary > 50000 THEN 'High'
        WHEN salary > 30000 THEN 'Medium'
        ELSE 'Low'
     END AS salary_category
FROM employees;
```

Use EXISTS Operator with Subquery

```
SELECT employee_id, first_name
FROM employees e
WHERE EXISTS (
   SELECT 1
   FROM departments d
   WHERE e.department_id = d.department_id
   AND d.location_id = 1700
);
```

Use Scalar Subquery

```
SELECT employee_id, first_name, salary,
     (SELECT MAX(salary) FROM employees) AS max_salary
FROM employees;
```

Use Data Types (NUMBER, VARCHAR2, DATE)

```
SELECT employee_id, first_name, hire_date
FROM employees;
```

Use TO_DATE() Function

```
SELECT employee_id, first_name, hire_date
```

```
FROM employees
WHERE hire_date >= TO_DATE('2022-01-01', 'YYYY-MM-DD');
```

Use TO_CHAR() Function

```
SELECT employee_id, first_name, TO_CHAR(hire_date, 'DD-MON-YYYY') AS
hire_date_formatted
FROM employees;
```

Use TRIM() Function

```
SELECT employee_id, TRIM(last_name) AS last_name_trimmed
FROM employees;
```

Use CONCAT() Function

```
SELECT CONCAT(first_name, ' ', last_name) AS full_name
FROM employees;
```

Use SYSDATE for Current Date

```
SELECT employee_id, first_name, hire_date
FROM employees
WHERE hire_date = TRUNC(SYSDATE);
```

Use Dual Table

```
SELECT SYSDATE FROM DUAL;
```

Use Sequence in Insert Statements

```
INSERT INTO employees (employee_id, first_name, last_name)
VALUES (emp_id_seq.NEXTVAL, 'Jane', 'Doe');
```

Use Database Links

```
SELECT e.employee_id, e.first_name, d.department_name
FROM employees e, departments@remote_db d
WHERE e.department_id = d.department_id;
```

Use CREATE USER

```
CREATE USER new_user IDENTIFIED BY password123;
```

Use GRANT Privileges

```
GRANT SELECT, INSERT, UPDATE ON employees TO new_user;
```

Use REVOKE Privileges

```
REVOKE INSERT ON employees FROM new_user;
```

Use CREATE ROLE

```
CREATE ROLE hr_role;
GRANT SELECT, INSERT, UPDATE ON employees TO hr_role;
```

Use SET Operators (UNION, INTERSECT, MINUS)

```
SELECT employee_id, first_name, last_name FROM employees WHERE
department_id = 10
UNION
SELECT employee_id, first_name, last_name FROM employees WHERE
department_id = 20;
```

Use Flashback Queries

```
SELECT * FROM employees AS OF TIMESTAMP (SYSTIMESTAMP -
INTERVAL '1' HOUR) WHERE department_id = 30;
```

Use Analyze Table Command

```
ANALYZE TABLE employees COMPUTE STATISTICS;
```

Use Bitmap Indexes

```
CREATE BITMAP INDEX idx_dept_id ON employees(department_id);
```

Use External Tables

```
CREATE DIRECTORY ext_data AS '/path/to/external/files';
CREATE TABLE ext_employees
   (employee_id NUMBER,
    first_name VARCHAR2(50),
    last_name VARCHAR2(50))
   ORGANIZATION EXTERNAL
   (TYPE ORACLE_LOADER
    DEFAULT DIRECTORY ext_data
    ACCESS PARAMETERS
    (RECORDS DELIMITED BY NEWLINE
     FIELDS TERMINATED BY ','));
```

Use LISTAGG() Function

```
SELECT department_id, LISTAGG(first_name, ', ') WITHIN GROUP (ORDER
BY employee_id) AS employee_list
FROM employees
GROUP BY department_id;
```

Use ROWNUM Pseudo Column

```
SELECT * FROM employees WHERE ROWNUM <= 10;
```

Use Analyze Functions (DBMS_STATS)

```
EXEC DBMS_STATS.GATHER_TABLE_STATS('HR', 'employees');
```

Use Parallel Query

```
SELECT /*+ PARALLEL(employees, 4) */ * FROM employees WHERE
department_id = 10;
```

Use Merge Statement

```
MERGE INTO employees e
USING (
```

```
    SELECT employee_id, first_name, last_name FROM new_employees
) ne
ON (e.employee_id = ne.employee_id)
WHEN MATCHED THEN
    UPDATE SET e.first_name = ne.first_name, e.last_name = ne.last_name
WHEN NOT MATCHED THEN
    INSERT (employee_id, first_name, last_name)
    VALUES (ne.employee_id, ne.first_name, ne.last_name);
```

Use Pivot and Unpivot Queries

```
SELECT *
FROM (
    SELECT department_id, job_id, salary
    FROM employees
)
PIVOT (
    AVG(salary)
    FOR job_id IN ('SA_REP' AS sales_rep, 'HR_REP' AS hr_rep)
);
```

Use Analytical Views

```
CREATE MATERIALIZED VIEW mv_employee_stats
BUILD IMMEDIATE
REFRESH FAST ON COMMIT
AS
SELECT department_id, AVG(salary) AS avg_salary
FROM employees
GROUP BY department_id;
```

Use SQL Loader

```
SELECT first_name, last_name
FROM employees
```

```
WHERE REGEXP_LIKE(last_name, '^S.*$');
```

Use Full-Text Search (CONTAINS)

```
SELECT *
FROM employees
WHERE CONTAINS(last_name, 'Smith', 1) > 0;
```

Use Rollup and Cube Operations

```
SELECT department_id, job_id, SUM(salary) AS total_salary
FROM employees
GROUP BY ROLLUP(department_id, job_id);
```

Use Flashback Table

```
FLASHBACK TABLE employees TO TIMESTAMP (SYSTIMESTAMP -
INTERVAL '1' HOUR');
```

Use Bulk Collect and FORALL

```
DECLARE
   TYPE emp_tab_type IS TABLE OF employees%ROWTYPE;
   emp_tab emp_tab_type;
BEGIN
   SELECT * BULK COLLECT INTO emp_tab FROM employees WHERE
department_id = 10;
   FORALL i IN 1..emp_tab.COUNT
      INSERT INTO new_employees VALUES emp_tab(i);
END;
```

Use Oracle Text (Text Searching and Indexing)

```
CREATE INDEX idx_emp_text_search ON employees(last_name)
INDEXTYPE IS CTXSYS.CONTEXT;
```

Use Database Links

Create a database link to connect to a remote database

```
CREATE DATABASE LINK remote_db
CONNECT TO remote_user IDENTIFIED BY password
USING 'remote_db_tns';
```

Use Fine-Grained Access Control (FGAC)

```
-- Define a security policy to restrict access based on user roles
BEGIN
   DBMS_RLS.ADD_POLICY(
      object_schema => 'hr',
      object_name => 'employees',
      policy_name => 'hr_access_policy',
      function_schema => 'security_pkg',
      policy_function => 'security_pkg.check_access',
      statement_types => 'SELECT, INSERT, UPDATE, DELETE',
      update_check => TRUE
   );
END;
```

Use Workspace Manager

```
-- Create a new workspace for managing changes
BEGIN
   DBMS_WM.CreateWorkspace(workspace => 'my_workspace', description =>
'Development Workspace');
   DBMS_WM.SetWorkspace('my_workspace');
END;
```

Use SQL*Plus

```
SET SERVEROUTPUT ON
BEGIN
   DBMS_OUTPUT.PUT_LINE('Hello, SQLcl!');
END;
/
```

Use Materialized Views

Create a materialized view to store precomputed query results

```
CREATE MATERIALIZED VIEW mv_employee_stats
BUILD IMMEDIATE
REFRESH FAST ON COMMIT
AS
SELECT department_id, AVG(salary) AS avg_salary
FROM employees
GROUP BY department_id;
```

Use SQL Performance Tuning

Analyze and tune SQL queries using EXPLAIN PLAN and SQL Monitoring

```
EXPLAIN PLAN FOR
SELECT * FROM employees WHERE department_id = 20;
```

Use SQL Monitoring

```
SELECT sql_id, sql_text, executions, elapsed_time
FROM v$sql_monitor
WHERE sql_text LIKE '%employees%';
```

Use In-Memory Column Store

Enable In-Memory Column Store for faster query performance

```
ALTER TABLE employees INMEMORY;
```

Use JSON Support in Oracle

Store and query JSON data using Oracle's JSON functions

```
SELECT *
FROM employees
WHERE JSON_EXISTS(info, '$.skills[0]');
```

Use Multitenant Architecture

Connect to a pluggable database (PDB) in a multitenant architecture

```
CONNECT username/password@pdb_name
SELECT * FROM employees WHERE department_id = 30;
```

Use Oracle Cloud Database Services

Connect to Oracle Cloud database service using SQL Developer

```
CONNECT username/password@cloud_db_tns
SELECT * FROM employees WHERE job_id = 'MANAGER';
```

PL/SQL

Hello World Program

```
BEGIN
   DBMS_OUTPUT.PUT_LINE('Hello, World!');
END;
/
```

Declare and Initialize Variables

```
DECLARE
   x NUMBER := 10;
   y VARCHAR2(20) := 'Hello';
BEGIN
   DBMS_OUTPUT.PUT_LINE('Value of x: ' || x);
   DBMS_OUTPUT.PUT_LINE('Value of y: ' || y);
END;
/
```

Basic Arithmetic Operations

```
DECLARE
   a NUMBER := 25;
   b NUMBER := 7;
   result NUMBER;
BEGIN
   result := a + b;
```

```
    DBMS_OUTPUT.PUT_LINE('Sum: ' || result);
    result := a - b;
    DBMS_OUTPUT.PUT_LINE('Difference: ' || result);
    result := a * b;
    DBMS_OUTPUT.PUT_LINE('Product: ' || result);
    result := a / b;
    DBMS_OUTPUT.PUT_LINE('Quotient: ' || result);
END;
/
```

If-Else Statement

```
DECLARE
    age NUMBER := 20;
BEGIN
    IF age >= 18 THEN
        DBMS_OUTPUT.PUT_LINE('You are an adult.');
    ELSE
        DBMS_OUTPUT.PUT_LINE('You are a minor.');
    END IF;
END;
/
```

Case Statement

```
DECLARE
    day_of_week VARCHAR2(20) := 'Monday';
BEGIN
    CASE day_of_week
        WHEN 'Monday' THEN
            DBMS_OUTPUT.PUT_LINE('It''s Monday!');
        WHEN 'Friday' THEN
            DBMS_OUTPUT.PUT_LINE('It''s Friday!');
        ELSE
```

```
        DBMS_OUTPUT.PUT_LINE('It''s neither Monday nor Friday.');
    END CASE;
END;
/
```

Loop with EXIT WHEN

```
DECLARE
    i NUMBER := 1;
BEGIN
    LOOP
        DBMS_OUTPUT.PUT_LINE('Value of i: ' || i);
        i := i + 1;
        EXIT WHEN i > 5;
    END LOOP;
END;
/
```

For Loop

```
DECLARE
    total NUMBER := 0;
BEGIN
    FOR i IN 1..10 LOOP
        total := total + i;
    END LOOP;
    DBMS_OUTPUT.PUT_LINE('Sum of numbers from 1 to 10: ' || total);
END;
/
```

While Loop

```
DECLARE
    j NUMBER := 1;
BEGIN
```

```
   WHILE j <= 5 LOOP
      DBMS_OUTPUT.PUT_LINE('Value of j: ' || j);
      j := j + 1;
   END LOOP;
END;
/
```

Nested Loops (Print Multiplication Table)

```
DECLARE
   multiplier NUMBER;
   multiplicand NUMBER;
BEGIN
   FOR multiplier IN 1..10 LOOP
      FOR multiplicand IN 1..10 LOOP
         DBMS_OUTPUT.PUT_LINE(multiplier || ' * ' || multiplicand || ' = ' ||
multiplier * multiplicand);
      END LOOP;
      DBMS_OUTPUT.PUT_LINE('--------------------');
   END LOOP;
END;
/
```

Factorial of a Number

```
DECLARE
   num NUMBER := 5;
   factorial NUMBER := 1;
BEGIN
   FOR i IN 1..num LOOP
      factorial := factorial * i;
   END LOOP;
   DBMS_OUTPUT.PUT_LINE('Factorial of ' || num || ' is ' || factorial);
END;/
```

Fibonacci Series

```
DECLARE
   n NUMBER := 10;
   a NUMBER := 0;
   b NUMBER := 1;
   next_term NUMBER;
BEGIN
   DBMS_OUTPUT.PUT_LINE('Fibonacci Series:');
   FOR i IN 1..n LOOP
      DBMS_OUTPUT.PUT_LINE(a);
      next_term := a + b;
      a := b;
      b := next_term;
   END LOOP;
END;
/
```

Reverse a String

```
DECLARE
   str VARCHAR2(100) := 'Hello';
   reversed_str VARCHAR2(100);
BEGIN
   FOR i IN REVERSE 1..LENGTH(str) LOOP
      reversed_str := reversed_str || SUBSTR(str, i, 1);
   END LOOP;
   DBMS_OUTPUT.PUT_LINE('Reversed String: ' || reversed_str);
END;
/
```

Palindrome Check

```
DECLARE
```

```
    str VARCHAR2(100) := 'madam';
    reversed_str VARCHAR2(100);
    is_palindrome BOOLEAN := TRUE;
BEGIN
    FOR i IN REVERSE 1..LENGTH(str) LOOP
        reversed_str := reversed_str || SUBSTR(str, i, 1);
    END LOOP;
    IF str <> reversed_str THEN
        is_palindrome := FALSE;
    END IF;

    IF is_palindrome THEN
        DBMS_OUTPUT.PUT_LINE('''' || str || ''' is a palindrome.');
    ELSE
        DBMS_OUTPUT.PUT_LINE('''' || str || ''' is not a palindrome.');
    END IF;
END;
/
```

Sum of Digits

```
DECLARE
    num NUMBER := 12345;
    sum NUMBER := 0;
BEGIN
    WHILE num > 0 LOOP
        sum := sum + MOD(num, 10);
        num := TRUNC(num / 10);
    END LOOP;
    DBMS_OUTPUT.PUT_LINE('Sum of Digits: ' || sum);
END;
/
```

Armstrong Number Check

```
DECLARE
   num NUMBER := 153;
   temp NUMBER := num;
   digit NUMBER;
   sum NUMBER := 0;
BEGIN
   WHILE temp > 0 LOOP
      digit := MOD(temp, 10);
      sum := sum + POWER(digit, 3);
      temp := TRUNC(temp / 10);
   END LOOP;
   IF num = sum THEN
      DBMS_OUTPUT.PUT_LINE(num || ' is an Armstrong number.');
   ELSE
      DBMS_OUTPUT.PUT_LINE(num || ' is not an Armstrong number.');
   END IF;
END;
/
```

Prime Number Check

```
DECLARE
   num NUMBER := 17;
   is_prime BOOLEAN := TRUE;
BEGIN
   IF num <= 1 THEN
      is_prime := FALSE;
   ELSE
      FOR i IN 2..TRUNC(SQRT(num)) LOOP
         IF MOD(num, i) = 0 THEN
            is_prime := FALSE;
            EXIT;
```

```
         END IF;
      END LOOP;
   END IF;
   IF is_prime THEN
      DBMS_OUTPUT.PUT_LINE(num || ' is a prime number.');
   ELSE
      DBMS_OUTPUT.PUT_LINE(num || ' is not a prime number.');
   END IF;
END;
/
```

Find Maximum of Two Numbers

```
DECLARE
   a NUMBER := 10;
   b NUMBER := 20;
   max_number NUMBER;
BEGIN
   IF a > b THEN
      max_number := a;
   ELSE
      max_number := b;
   END IF;
   DBMS_OUTPUT.PUT_LINE('Maximum of ' || a || ' and ' || b || ' is: ' ||
max_number);
END;
/
```

Find Maximum of Three Numbers

```
DECLARE
   x NUMBER := 30;
   y NUMBER := 50;
   z NUMBER := 20;
```

```
   max_number NUMBER;
BEGIN
   max_number := GREATEST(x, y, z);
   DBMS_OUTPUT.PUT_LINE('Maximum of ' || x || ', ' || y || ', and ' || z || ' is: ' ||
max_number);
END;
/
```

Find Minimum of Two Numbers

```
DECLARE
   a NUMBER := 15;
   b NUMBER := 8;
   min_number NUMBER;
BEGIN
   IF a < b THEN
      min_number := a;
   ELSE
      min_number := b;
   END IF;
   DBMS_OUTPUT.PUT_LINE('Minimum of ' || a || ' and ' || b || ' is: ' ||
min_number);
END;
/
```

Swap Two Numbers

```
DECLARE
   x NUMBER := 10;
   y NUMBER := 20;
   temp NUMBER;
BEGIN
   DBMS_OUTPUT.PUT_LINE('Before swapping - x: ' || x || ', y: ' || y);
   temp := x;
```

```
    x := y;
    y := temp;
    DBMS_OUTPUT.PUT_LINE('After swapping - x: ' || x || ', y: ' || y);
END;
/
```

Linear Search

```
DECLARE
    numbers SYS.ODCINUMBERLIST := SYS.ODCINUMBERLIST(10, 20, 30,
40, 50);
    target NUMBER := 30;
    found BOOLEAN := FALSE;
BEGIN
    FOR i IN 1..numbers.COUNT LOOP
        IF numbers(i) = target THEN
            found := TRUE;
            EXIT;
        END IF;
    END LOOP;
    IF found THEN
        DBMS_OUTPUT.PUT_LINE('Target ' || target || ' found.');
    ELSE
        DBMS_OUTPUT.PUT_LINE('Target ' || target || ' not found.');
    END IF;
END;
/
```

Binary Search (assuming array is sorted)

```
DECLARE
    numbers SYS.ODCINUMBERLIST := SYS.ODCINUMBERLIST(10, 20, 30,
40, 50);
    target NUMBER := 30;
```

```
   found BOOLEAN := FALSE;
   low NUMBER := 1;
   high NUMBER := numbers.COUNT;
   mid NUMBER;
BEGIN
   WHILE low <= high LOOP
      mid := (low + high) / 2;
      IF numbers(mid) = target THEN
         found := TRUE;
         EXIT;
      ELSIF numbers(mid) < target THEN
         low := mid + 1;
      ELSE
         high := mid - 1;
      END IF;
   END LOOP;
   IF found THEN
      DBMS_OUTPUT.PUT_LINE('Target ' || target || ' found.');
   ELSE
      DBMS_OUTPUT.PUT_LINE('Target ' || target || ' not found.');
   END IF;
END;
/
```

Bubble Sort

```
DECLARE
   numbers SYS.ODCINUMBERLIST := SYS.ODCINUMBERLIST(64, 34, 25,
12, 22, 11, 90);
   temp NUMBER;
BEGIN
   FOR i IN 1..numbers.COUNT-1 LOOP
      FOR j IN 1..numbers.COUNT-i LOOP
```

```
        IF numbers(j) > numbers(j+1) THEN
          temp := numbers(j);
          numbers(j) := numbers(j+1);
          numbers(j+1) := temp;
        END IF;
      END LOOP;
  END LOOP;
  DBMS_OUTPUT.PUT_LINE('Sorted Array: ' || numbers);
END;
```

Selection Sort

```
DECLARE
  numbers SYS.ODCINUMBERLIST := SYS.ODCINUMBERLIST(64, 34, 25,
12, 22, 11, 90);
  min_idx NUMBER;
  temp NUMBER;
BEGIN
  FOR i IN 1..numbers.COUNT-1 LOOP
    min_idx := i;
    FOR j IN i+1..numbers.COUNT LOOP
      IF numbers(j) < numbers(min_idx) THEN
        min_idx := j;
      END IF;
    END LOOP;
    IF min_idx != i THEN
      temp := numbers(i);
      numbers(i) := numbers(min_idx);
      numbers(min_idx) := temp;
    END IF;
  END LOOP;
  DBMS_OUTPUT.PUT_LINE('Sorted Array: ' || numbers);
END;/
```

Insertion Sort

```
DECLARE
   numbers SYS.ODCINUMBERLIST := SYS.ODCINUMBERLIST(64, 34, 25,
12, 22, 11, 90);
   key NUMBER;
   j NUMBER;
BEGIN
   FOR i IN 2..numbers.COUNT LOOP
      key := numbers(i);
      j := i - 1;

      WHILE j > 0 AND numbers(j) > key LOOP
         numbers(j + 1) := numbers(j);
         j := j - 1;
      END LOOP;
      numbers(j + 1) := key;
   END LOOP;
   DBMS_OUTPUT.PUT_LINE('Sorted Array: ' || numbers);
END;
/
```

Implement Stack using PL/SQL

```
CREATE OR REPLACE TYPE stack AS OBJECT (
   elements SYS.ODCINUMBERLIST,
   MEMBER PROCEDURE push(element NUMBER),
   MEMBER PROCEDURE pop,
   MEMBER FUNCTION isEmpty RETURN BOOLEAN
);
/
CREATE OR REPLACE TYPE BODY stack AS
   MEMBER PROCEDURE push(element NUMBER) IS
```

```
  BEGIN
    elements.EXTEND;
    elements(elements.LAST) := element;
  END;
  MEMBER PROCEDURE pop IS
  BEGIN
    IF NOT isEmpty THEN
      elements.DELETE(elements.LAST);
    END IF;
  END;
  MEMBER FUNCTION isEmpty RETURN BOOLEAN IS
  BEGIN
    RETURN elements.COUNT = 0;
  END;
END;
/
```

Usage Example of Stack

```
DECLARE
  s stack := stack(SYS.ODCINUMBERLIST());
BEGIN
  s.push(10);
  s.push(20);
  s.push(30);
  DBMS_OUTPUT.PUT_LINE('Stack is empty: ' || s.isEmpty);
  s.pop;
  DBMS_OUTPUT.PUT_LINE('Stack is empty after pop: ' || s.isEmpty);
END;
/
```

Implement Queue using PL/SQL

```
CREATE OR REPLACE TYPE queue AS OBJECT (
```

```
    elements SYS.ODCINUMBERLIST,
    MEMBER PROCEDURE enqueue(element NUMBER),
    MEMBER PROCEDURE dequeue,
    MEMBER FUNCTION isEmpty RETURN BOOLEAN
);
/

CREATE OR REPLACE TYPE BODY queue AS
    MEMBER PROCEDURE enqueue(element NUMBER) IS
    BEGIN
        elements.EXTEND;
        elements(elements.LAST) := element;
    END;
    MEMBER PROCEDURE dequeue IS
    BEGIN
        IF NOT isEmpty THEN
            elements.DELETE(1);
        END IF;
    END;
    MEMBER FUNCTION isEmpty RETURN BOOLEAN IS
    BEGIN
        RETURN elements.COUNT = 0;
    END;
END;
/
```

Usage Example of Queue

```
DECLARE
    q queue := queue(SYS.ODCINUMBERLIST());
BEGIN
    q.enqueue(10);
    q.enqueue(20);
```

```
    q.enqueue(30);
    DBMS_OUTPUT.PUT_LINE('Queue is empty: ' || q.isEmpty);
    q.dequeue;
    DBMS_OUTPUT.PUT_LINE('Queue is empty after dequeue: ' || q.isEmpty);
END;
/
```

Implement Linked List using PL/SQL (simplified version)

```
CREATE OR REPLACE TYPE node AS OBJECT (
    value NUMBER,
    next_node node
);
/
```

Usage Example of Linked List

```
DECLARE
    n1 node := node(10, NULL);
    n2 node := node(20, NULL);
BEGIN
    n1.next_node := n2;
    DBMS_OUTPUT.PUT_LINE('Value of first node: ' || n1.value);
    DBMS_OUTPUT.PUT_LINE('Value of second node: ' || n1.next_node.value);
END;
/
```

Implement Binary Tree using PL/SQL

```
CREATE OR REPLACE TYPE TreeNode AS OBJECT (
    value NUMBER,
    left_child TreeNode,
    right_child TreeNode
);
/
```

Recursive Procedures to insert a value into a Binary Tree

```
CREATE OR REPLACE PROCEDURE insertIntoBinaryTree(root IN OUT
TreeNode, value_to_insert NUMBER) AS
BEGIN
   IF root IS NULL THEN
      root := TreeNode(value_to_insert, NULL, NULL);
   ELSIF value_to_insert < root.value THEN
      insertIntoBinaryTree(root.left_child, value_to_insert);
   ELSE
      insertIntoBinaryTree(root.right_child, value_to_insert);
   END IF;
END;
/
```

Cursor with Loop to traverse and print Binary Tree (Inorder Traversal)

```
CREATE OR REPLACE PROCEDURE printBinaryTreeInorder(root IN
TreeNode) AS
   CURSOR tree_cursor IS
      SELECT value, left_child, right_child
      FROM TreeNode
      WHERE value = root.value;
   node TreeNode;
BEGIN
   OPEN tree_cursor;
   FETCH tree_cursor INTO node;
   CLOSE tree_cursor;
   IF node IS NOT NULL THEN
      printBinaryTreeInorder(node.left_child);
      DBMS_OUTPUT.PUT_LINE(node.value);
      printBinaryTreeInorder(node.right_child);
   END IF;END;/
```

Cursor with Parameter to traverse and print Binary Tree (Preorder Traversal)

```
CREATE OR REPLACE PROCEDURE printBinaryTreePreorder(root IN
TreeNode) AS
  PROCEDURE traverse(node IN TreeNode) IS
  BEGIN
    IF node IS NOT NULL THEN
      DBMS_OUTPUT.PUT_LINE(node.value);
      traverse(node.left_child);
      traverse(node.right_child);
    END IF;
  END;
BEGIN
  traverse(root);
END;
/
```

Exception Handling (Divide by Zero)

```
DECLARE
  dividend NUMBER := 10;
  divisor NUMBER := 0;
  result NUMBER;
BEGIN
  result := dividend / divisor;
EXCEPTION
  WHEN ZERO_DIVIDE THEN
    DBMS_OUTPUT.PUT_LINE('Error: Divide by zero');
END;
/
```

Raise Application Error

```
DECLARE
```

```
    my_error EXCEPTION;
BEGIN
    RAISE my_error;
EXCEPTION
    WHEN my_error THEN
        RAISE_APPLICATION_ERROR(-20001, 'Custom error occurred');
END;
/
```

User-Defined Exception

```
DECLARE
    my_exception EXCEPTION;
BEGIN
    IF SYSDATE > TO_DATE('2025-01-01', 'YYYY-MM-DD') THEN
        RAISE my_exception;
    END IF;
EXCEPTION
    WHEN my_exception THEN
        DBMS_OUTPUT.PUT_LINE('Custom exception occurred');
END;
/
```

Handle NO_DATA_FOUND Exception

```
DECLARE
    v_name VARCHAR2(50);
BEGIN
    SELECT first_name
    INTO v_name
    FROM employees
    WHERE employee_id = 1000;
    DBMS_OUTPUT.PUT_LINE('Employee Name: ' || v_name);
EXCEPTION
```

```
    WHEN NO_DATA_FOUND THEN
        DBMS_OUTPUT.PUT_LINE('Employee not found');
END;/
```

Handle DUP_VAL_ON_INDEX Exception

```
DECLARE
    v_emp_id NUMBER := 101;
BEGIN
    INSERT INTO employees (employee_id, first_name, last_name)
    VALUES (v_emp_id, 'John', 'Doe');
EXCEPTION
    WHEN DUP_VAL_ON_INDEX THEN
        DBMS_OUTPUT.PUT_LINE('Duplicate employee ID: ' || v_emp_id);
END;
/
```

Implement Packages with Procedures and Functions

```
CREATE OR REPLACE PACKAGE my_package AS
    PROCEDURE procedure1;
    FUNCTION function1 RETURN NUMBER;
END my_package;
/
CREATE OR REPLACE PACKAGE BODY my_package AS
    PROCEDURE procedure1 IS
    BEGIN
        DBMS_OUTPUT.PUT_LINE('Executing procedure1');
    END;

    FUNCTION function1 RETURN NUMBER IS
    BEGIN
        RETURN 10;
    END;
```

```
END my_package;
/
```

Overloading Procedures

```
CREATE OR REPLACE PACKAGE my_package AS
   PROCEDURE procedure2(p_num NUMBER);
   PROCEDURE procedure2(p_str VARCHAR2);
END my_package;
/
CREATE OR REPLACE PACKAGE BODY my_package AS
   PROCEDURE procedure2(p_num NUMBER) IS
   BEGIN
      DBMS_OUTPUT.PUT_LINE('Number parameter: ' || p_num);
   END;

   PROCEDURE procedure2(p_str VARCHAR2) IS
   BEGIN
      DBMS_OUTPUT.PUT_LINE('String parameter: ' || p_str);
   END;
END my_package;
/
```

Overloading Functions

```
CREATE OR REPLACE PACKAGE my_package AS
   FUNCTION sum(a NUMBER, b NUMBER) RETURN NUMBER;
   FUNCTION sum(a VARCHAR2, b VARCHAR2) RETURN VARCHAR2;
END my_package;
/
CREATE OR REPLACE PACKAGE BODY my_package AS
   FUNCTION sum(a NUMBER, b NUMBER) RETURN NUMBER IS
   BEGIN
      RETURN a + b;
```

```
    END;

    FUNCTION sum(a VARCHAR2, b VARCHAR2) RETURN VARCHAR2 IS
    BEGIN
        RETURN a || ' ' || b;
    END;
END my_package;
/
```

Implement Triggers (BEFORE INSERT, AFTER UPDATE, INSTEAD OF DELETE)

```
CREATE OR REPLACE TRIGGER before_employee_insert
BEFORE INSERT ON employees
FOR EACH ROW
BEGIN
    :NEW.creation_date := SYSDATE;
END;
/

CREATE OR REPLACE TRIGGER after_employee_update
AFTER UPDATE OF salary ON employees
FOR EACH ROW
BEGIN
    IF :NEW.salary > :OLD.salary THEN
        DBMS_OUTPUT.PUT_LINE('Salary increased');
    ELSIF :NEW.salary < :OLD.salary THEN
        DBMS_OUTPUT.PUT_LINE('Salary decreased');
    END IF;
END;
/
CREATE OR REPLACE TRIGGER instead_of_employee_delete
INSTEAD OF DELETE ON employees
```

```
BEGIN
   -- Custom delete logic here
   NULL;
END;
/
```

Use Sequences

```
CREATE SEQUENCE emp_id_seq START WITH 1001 INCREMENT BY 1;
/
```

Use Synonyms

```
CREATE SYNONYM emp FOR employees;
/
```

Use Views

```
CREATE VIEW emp_view AS
SELECT employee_id, first_name, last_name, salary
FROM employees
WHERE department_id = 10;
/
```

Use Indexes

```
CREATE INDEX idx_lastname ON employees(last_name);
/
```

Implement Database Transactions

```
DECLARE
   v_emp_id NUMBER := 1001;
BEGIN
   INSERT INTO employees (employee_id, first_name, last_name)
   VALUES (v_emp_id, 'Jane', 'Doe');
   COMMIT;
EXCEPTION
   WHEN OTHERS THEN
```

```
        ROLLBACK;
END;
/
```

Savepoints in Transactions

```
DECLARE
    v_emp_id NUMBER := 1002;
BEGIN
    INSERT INTO employees (employee_id, first_name, last_name)
    VALUES (v_emp_id, 'Mike', 'Smith');
    SAVEPOINT before_update;
    UPDATE employees
    SET salary = salary * 1.1
    WHERE employee_id = v_emp_id;
```

Rollback to savepoint if condition not met

```
    IF SQL%ROWCOUNT = 0 THEN
        ROLLBACK TO before_update;
    END IF;
    COMMIT;
EXCEPTION
    WHEN OTHERS THEN
        ROLLBACK;
END;
/
```

Bulk Collect and FORALL

```
DECLARE
   TYPE emp_list IS TABLE OF employees%ROWTYPE;
   l_emps emp_list;
BEGIN
   SELECT *
   BULK COLLECT INTO l_emps
   FROM employees
   WHERE department_id = 20;
   FORALL i IN 1..l_emps.COUNT
      UPDATE employees
      SET salary = salary * 1.05
      WHERE employee_id = l_emps(i).employee_id;

   COMMIT;
END;
/
```

Dynamic SQL (EXECUTE IMMEDIATE)

```
DECLARE
   v_sql VARCHAR2(100);
   v_count NUMBER;
BEGIN
   v_sql := 'SELECT COUNT(*) FROM employees';
   EXECUTE IMMEDIATE v_sql INTO v_count;
   DBMS_OUTPUT.PUT_LINE('Total Employees: ' || v_count);
END;
/
```

PL/SQL Record Types

```
DECLARE
   TYPE emp_record IS RECORD (
```

```
        emp_id NUMBER,
        emp_name VARCHAR2(100),
        emp_salary NUMBER
    );
    v_employee emp_record;
BEGIN
    v_employee.emp_id := 101;
    v_employee.emp_name := 'John Doe';
    v_employee.emp_salary := 5000;
    DBMS_OUTPUT.PUT_LINE('Employee ID: ' || v_employee.emp_id || ', Name:
' || v_employee.emp_name);
END;
/
```

PL/SQL Collections (Associative Arrays, Nested Tables, VARRAYs)

```
DECLARE
    TYPE string_array IS TABLE OF VARCHAR2(100);
    v_names string_array := string_array('John', 'Doe', 'Jane', 'Smith');
BEGIN
    FOR i IN 1..v_names.COUNT LOOP
        DBMS_OUTPUT.PUT_LINE('Name: ' || v_names(i));
    END LOOP;
END;
/
```

Use BULK COLLECT with Collections

```
DECLARE
    TYPE emp_records IS TABLE OF employees%ROWTYPE;
    v_emps emp_records;
BEGIN
    SELECT * BULK COLLECT INTO v_emps FROM employees WHERE
department_id = 20;
```

```
   FOR i IN 1..v_emps.COUNT LOOP
      DBMS_OUTPUT.PUT_LINE('Employee Name: ' || v_emps(i).first_name || ' '
|| v_emps(i).last_name);
   END LOOP;
END;
/
```

Use FORALL with Collections

```
DECLARE
   TYPE emp_ids IS TABLE OF employees.employee_id%TYPE;
   v_emp_ids emp_ids := emp_ids(101, 102, 103);
BEGIN
   FORALL i IN 1..v_emp_ids.COUNT
      UPDATE employees
      SET salary = salary * 1.05
      WHERE employee_id = v_emp_ids(i);
   COMMIT;
END;
/
```

Implement Database Cursors (Implicit Cursor)

```
DECLARE
   v_first_name employees.first_name%TYPE;
BEGIN
   SELECT first_name INTO v_first_name FROM employees WHERE
employee_id = 101;
   DBMS_OUTPUT.PUT_LINE('Employee First Name: ' || v_first_name);
END;
/
```

Use REF CURSOR

```
DECLARE
```

```
    TYPE emp_cursor IS REF CURSOR;
    v_emp_cursor emp_cursor;
    v_emp_id employees.employee_id%TYPE;
    v_first_name employees.first_name%TYPE;
BEGIN
    OPEN v_emp_cursor FOR SELECT employee_id, first_name FROM
employees WHERE department_id = 30;
    LOOP
        FETCH v_emp_cursor INTO v_emp_id, v_first_name;
        EXIT WHEN v_emp_cursor%NOTFOUND;
        DBMS_OUTPUT.PUT_LINE('Employee ID: ' || v_emp_id || ', First Name: ' ||
v_first_name);
    END LOOP;
    CLOSE v_emp_cursor;
END;
/
```

Cursor Attributes (%FOUND, %NOTFOUND, %ROWCOUNT)

```
DECLARE
    CURSOR emp_cursor IS SELECT * FROM employees WHERE
department_id = 20;
    v_emp_rec employees%ROWTYPE;
BEGIN
    OPEN emp_cursor;
    LOOP
        FETCH emp_cursor INTO v_emp_rec;
        EXIT WHEN emp_cursor%NOTFOUND;
        DBMS_OUTPUT.PUT_LINE('Employee ID: ' || v_emp_rec.employee_id || ',
Name: ' || v_emp_rec.first_name);
    END LOOP;
    CLOSE emp_cursor;
    IF emp_cursor%FOUND THEN
```

```
DBMS_OUTPUT.PUT_LINE('Total Employees: ' || emp_cursor%ROWCOUNT);
  END IF;
END;
/
```

Analytic Functions (ROW_NUMBER, RANK, DENSE_RANK)

```
DECLARE
  CURSOR emp_cursor IS
    SELECT employee_id, first_name, salary,
        ROW_NUMBER() OVER (ORDER BY salary DESC) AS rn,
        RANK() OVER (ORDER BY salary DESC) AS rnk,
        DENSE_RANK() OVER (ORDER BY salary DESC) AS drnk
    FROM employees
    WHERE department_id = 10;
  v_emp_id employees.employee_id%TYPE;
  v_first_name employees.first_name%TYPE;
  v_salary employees.salary%TYPE;
  v_row_num NUMBER;
  v_rank NUMBER;
  v_dense_rank NUMBER;
BEGIN
  OPEN emp_cursor;
  LOOP
    FETCH emp_cursor INTO v_emp_id, v_first_name, v_salary, v_row_num,
v_rank, v_dense_rank;
    EXIT WHEN emp_cursor%NOTFOUND;
    DBMS_OUTPUT.PUT_LINE('Employee ID: ' || v_emp_id || ', Name: ' ||
v_first_name ||
              ', Salary: ' || v_salary || ', Row Number: ' || v_row_num ||
              ', Rank: ' || v_rank || ', Dense Rank: ' || v_dense_rank);
  END LOOP;
  CLOSE emp_cursor;
END;/
```

Use DBMS_OUTPUT.PUT_LINE for Debugging

```
DECLARE
   v_name VARCHAR2(100) := 'John Doe';
BEGIN
   DBMS_OUTPUT.PUT_LINE('Employee Name: ' || v_name);
END;
/
```

Implement Error Logging

```
DECLARE
   v_result NUMBER;
BEGIN
   -- Perform some operations that may raise an error
   v_result := 10 / 0; -- Division by zero error
EXCEPTION
   WHEN OTHERS THEN
      INSERT INTO error_log (error_message, error_timestamp)
      VALUES (SQLERRM, SYSTIMESTAMP);
      DBMS_OUTPUT.PUT_LINE('Error occurred: ' || SQLERRM);
END;
/
```

Implement Row-level Security

```
CREATE OR REPLACE FUNCTION hr_security_predicate (
   schema_name IN VARCHAR2,
   table_name IN VARCHAR2
) RETURN VARCHAR2
IS
   v_predicate VARCHAR2(100);
BEGIN
   v_predicate := 'department_id = SYS_CONTEXT(''USERENV'',
```

```
"CURRENT_USER_DEPT_ID")';
   RETURN v_predicate;
END;
/
BEGIN
   DBMS_RLS.ADD_POLICY(
      object_schema => 'hr',
      object_name => 'employees',
      policy_name => 'hr_security_policy',
      policy_function => 'hr_security_predicate',
      statement_types => 'SELECT, INSERT, UPDATE, DELETE',
      update_check => TRUE
   );
END;
/
```

Use Regular Expressions in PL/SQL

```
DECLARE
   v_string VARCHAR2(100) := 'Hello123World';
BEGIN
   IF REGEXP_LIKE(v_string, '[0-9]+') THEN
      DBMS_OUTPUT.PUT_LINE('String contains digits');
   ELSE
      DBMS_OUTPUT.PUT_LINE('String does not contain digits');
   END IF;
END;
/
```

Implement Fine-Grained Access Control (FGAC)

```
BEGIN
   DBMS_SCHEDULER.CREATE_JOB(
      job_name => 'my_job',
```

```
        job_type => 'PLSQL_BLOCK',
        job_action => 'BEGIN DBMS_OUTPUT.PUT_LINE(''Scheduled Job
Running''); END;',
        start_date => SYSTIMESTAMP,
        repeat_interval => 'FREQ=HOURLY; INTERVAL=1',
        enabled => TRUE
    );
END;
/
```

Use DBMS_JOB for Job Scheduling (Legacy)

```
DECLARE
    v_job NUMBER;
BEGIN
    DBMS_JOB.SUBMIT(
        job => v_job,
        what => 'BEGIN DBMS_OUTPUT.PUT_LINE(''Legacy Job Running'');
END;',
        next_date => SYSTIMESTAMP,
        interval => 'SYSDATE + 1'
    );
    COMMIT;
END;
/
```

Implement Global Temporary Tables

```
CREATE GLOBAL TEMPORARY TABLE temp_employees (
    employee_id NUMBER,
    first_name VARCHAR2(50),
    last_name VARCHAR2(50)
) ON COMMIT DELETE ROWS;
```

Implement Pipelined Table Functions

```
CREATE OR REPLACE TYPE emp_info_type AS OBJECT (
   employee_id NUMBER,
   first_name VARCHAR2(50),
   last_name VARCHAR2(50)
);
/
CREATE OR REPLACE TYPE emp_info_table AS TABLE OF emp_info_type;
/
CREATE OR REPLACE FUNCTION get_employees_info
RETURN emp_info_table PIPELINED
IS
   v_emp_info emp_info_type;
BEGIN
   FOR emp_rec IN (SELECT employee_id, first_name, last_name FROM
employees)
   LOOP
      v_emp_info := emp_info_type(emp_rec.employee_id, emp_rec.first_name,
emp_rec.last_name);
      PIPE ROW (v_emp_info);
   END LOOP;
   RETURN;
END;
/
```

Use PRAGMA AUTONOMOUS_TRANSACTION

```
DECLARE
   PRAGMA AUTONOMOUS_TRANSACTION;
BEGIN
   INSERT INTO audit_log (action, action_timestamp)
   VALUES ('Employee Added', SYSTIMESTAMP);
   COMMIT;
```

```
END;
/
```

Use UTL_FILE for File I/O

```
DECLARE
   v_file_handle UTL_FILE.FILE_TYPE;
   v_file_name VARCHAR2(100) := 'output_file.txt';
BEGIN
   v_file_handle := UTL_FILE.FOPEN('DIR_TEMP', v_file_name, 'W');
   UTL_FILE.PUT_LINE(v_file_handle, 'Hello, this is a test line.');
   UTL_FILE.FCLOSE(v_file_handle);
END;
/
```

Implement Hash Functions

```
DECLARE
   v_input VARCHAR2(100) := 'Hello World';
   v_hash RAW(32);
BEGIN
   v_hash := DBMS_CRYPTO.HASH(UTL_RAW.CAST_TO_RAW(v_input),
DBMS_CRYPTO.HASH_MD5);
   DBMS_OUTPUT.PUT_LINE('Hash Value (MD5): ' ||
UTL_RAW.CAST_TO_VARCHAR2(v_hash));
END;
/
```

Implement Cryptographic Functions

```
DECLARE
   v_plain_text VARCHAR2(100) := 'Secret Message';
   v_key RAW(32);
   v_encrypted RAW(2000);
   v_decrypted VARCHAR2(100);
```

```
BEGIN
   v_key := DBMS_CRYPTO.RANDOMBYTES(32);
   v_encrypted :=
DBMS_CRYPTO.ENCRYPT(UTL_RAW.CAST_TO_RAW(v_plain_text),
DBMS_CRYPTO.DES_CBC_PKCS5, v_key);
   v_decrypted :=
UTL_RAW.CAST_TO_VARCHAR2(DBMS_CRYPTO.DECRYPT(v_encrypted
, DBMS_CRYPTO.DES_CBC_PKCS5, v_key));
   DBMS_OUTPUT.PUT_LINE('Decrypted Text: ' || v_decrypted);
END;
/
```

Implement XML Parsing and Generation

```
DECLARE
   v_xml XMLTYPE;
BEGIN
   v_xml :=
XMLTYPE('<employees><employee><id>101</id><name>John</name></empl
oyee></employees>');
   DBMS_OUTPUT.PUT_LINE('Employee ID: ' ||
v_xml.extract('/employees/employee/id').getStringVal());
   DBMS_OUTPUT.PUT_LINE('Employee Name: ' ||
v_xml.extract('/employees/employee/name').getStringVal());
END;
/
```

Implement JSON Parsing and Generation

```
DECLARE
   v_json VARCHAR2(4000) := '{"employee_id": 101, "first_name": "John",
"last_name": "Doe"}';
   v_employee_id NUMBER;
   v_first_name VARCHAR2(50);
```

```
    v_last_name VARCHAR2(50);
BEGIN
    v_employee_id := JSON_VALUE(v_json, '$.employee_id');
    v_first_name := JSON_VALUE(v_json, '$.first_name');
    v_last_name := JSON_VALUE(v_json, '$.last_name');
    DBMS_OUTPUT.PUT_LINE('Employee ID: ' || v_employee_id);
    DBMS_OUTPUT.PUT_LINE('First Name: ' || v_first_name);
    DBMS_OUTPUT.PUT_LINE('Last Name: ' || v_last_name);
END;
/
```

Implement RESTful Web Services in PL/SQL

```
DECLARE
    v_clob CLOB;
    v_blob BLOB;
BEGIN
    INSERT INTO my_table (id, clob_column, blob_column)
    VALUES (1, EMPTY_CLOB(), EMPTY_BLOB())
    RETURNING clob_column, blob_column INTO v_clob, v_blob;
        DBMS_LOB.WRITEAPPEND(v_clob, LENGTH('Some text'), 'Some text');
    DBMS_LOB.APPEND(v_blob, HEXTORAW('012345'));
END;
/
```

Implement Data Encryption and Decryption

```
DECLARE
    v_plain_text VARCHAR2(100) := 'Secret Message';
    v_encrypted_raw RAW(2000);
    v_decrypted_text VARCHAR2(100);
BEGIN
    v_encrypted_raw :=
DBMS_CRYPTO.ENCRYPT(UTL_RAW.CAST_TO_RAW(v_plain_text),
```

```
DBMS_CRYPTO.AES_CBC_PKCS5, UTL_RAW.CAST_TO_RAW('my_key'));
   v_decrypted_text :=
UTL_RAW.CAST_TO_VARCHAR2(DBMS_CRYPTO.DECRYPT(v_encrypted
_raw, DBMS_CRYPTO.AES_CBC_PKCS5,
UTL_RAW.CAST_TO_RAW('my_key')));
   DBMS_OUTPUT.PUT_LINE('Decrypted Text: ' || v_decrypted_text);
END;
/
```

www.ingramcontent.com/pod-product-compliance
Lightning Source LLC
LaVergne TN
LVHW050346160826
845677LV00014B/3825

* 9 7 8 9 3 3 4 0 5 2 4 3 5 *